Ali and Annie's Guide to...

Coping with Separation and Divorce

Jilly Hunt

raintree

a Capstone company — publishers for children

Raintree is an imprint of Capstone Global Library Limited, a company incorporated in England and Wales having its registered office at 264 Banbury Road, Oxford, OX2 7DY – Registered company number: 6695582

www.raintree.co.uk
myorders@raintree.co.uk

Edited by Clare Lewis and Helen Cox Cannons
Designed by Dynamo
Original illustrations © Capstone Global Library Limited 2019
Picture research by Dynamo
Production by Tori Abraham
Originated by Capstone Global Library Limited
Printed and bound in India

ISBN 978 1 4747 7303 4 (hardback)
22 21 20 19 18
10 9 8 7 6 5 4 3 2 1

ISBN 978 1 4747 7309 6 (paperback)
23 22 21 20 19
10 9 8 7 6 5 4 3 2 1

British Library Cataloguing in Publication Data
A full catalogue record for this book is available from the British Library.

Acknowledgements
We would like to thank the following for permission to reproduce photographs:
Getty Images: E+/AmpH, 20, E+/fzant, 15, E+/PeopleImages, 4, 16, 19 Bottom Right, E+/shapecharge, 22, E+/SolStock, 24, E+/Weekend Images Inc., 23, iStock/agalma, 18 Right, iStock/AntonioGuillem, 7 Bottom Right, iStock/AzmanL, 17, iStock/DGLimages, 26 Right, iStock/gradyreese, 27 Bottom Right, iStock/Jovanmandic, 21, iStock/karelnoppe, 14, iStock/monkeybusinessimages, Cover, 1, 11, iStock/Rawpixel, 13, iStock/sakkmesterke, 5 Top Right, iStock/ Sladic, 9, iStock/tatyana_tomsickova, 28, iStock/Toxitz, 12, iStock/vadimguzhva, 6 Right, 10, iStock/Wavebreakmedia, 8, OJO Images/ Robert Daly, 25.

We would like to thank Charlotte Mitchell for her invaluable help with the preparation of this book.

Every effort has been made to contact copyright holders of material reproduced in this book. Any omissions will be rectified in subsequent printings if notice is given to the publisher.

All the internet addresses (URLs) given in this book were valid at the time of going to press. However, due to the dynamic nature of the internet, some addresses may have changed, or sites may have changed or ceased to exist since publication. While the author and publisher regret any inconvenience this may cause readers, no responsibility for any such changes can be accepted by either the author or the publisher.

Contents

I'm Ali! Look out for our helpful tips throughout the book.

Hi! I'm Annie and this is my dog, Charlie.

Some words are shown in bold, **like this**. You can find out what they mean by looking in the glossary.

What is separation?

Sometimes parents don't get on together. They may argue a lot. In their spare time, they may prefer to do different things. They may decide to have some time living apart. This is called separation.

TIP

Don't feel like you need to take sides and choose between your parents.

Married and unmarried couples can find the decision to separate a difficult one.

▲ A counsellor can help a couple understand each other better.

A couple with problems may see a **relationship counsellor**. The counsellor helps them to talk about their problems. This might help the couple find solutions to their problems. Some couples may decide to try to keep living together. Others may decide they prefer to live apart.

What is divorce?

A **lawyer** does the paperwork for the coup to sign that makes their divorce legal.

Divorce is when a married couple decide to stop being married to each other. Just as getting married is a **legal** thing, so is getting divorced. A married couple needs to sign paperwork to say they both want to be single again.

TIP

Parents divorce each other, not their children. They still love you just the same as they always have.

If your parents are getting divorced, they need to decide who you will live with. They also need to decide how often you will see or stay with each parent. If they can't agree, they may need to go to **court**. Then a **judge** will decide what is best for you.

▲ Parents need to have lots of important conversations if they are getting divorced.

Why do parents split up?

Parents split up for lots of different reasons. They just might not get on with each other any more. One parent may have met someone else they want to spend their time with. Or they might have more difficult issues to work out. They think they will be happier if they live apart.

▲ Unhappy parents may argue a lot.

Your parents may not get on with each other but they still love you. It's not your fault if your parents are splitting up. It's important not to blame yourself.

Your parents' feelings

TIP

Separation or divorce is a difficult time for everyone involved. Your parents might be feeling a mix of **emotions**. They might be feeling angry with each other. They might be sad or lonely. They might feel guilty that they are upsetting the family.

Your parents might find it hard to adjust to the change too. But it's not your **responsibility** to look after them. You can help by trying to understand and by being extra kind and helpful.

▶ Your parents will be worried about you too.

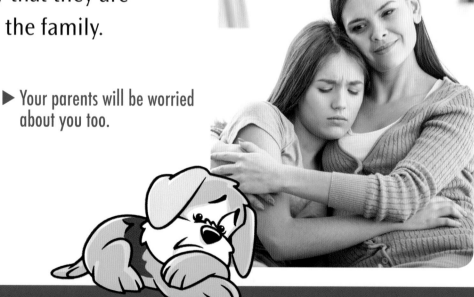

Your parents will have lots of things to sort out. This can be difficult if they are also feeling upset. Your parents may feel extra busy or stressed. They might be more grumpy or tearful than normal.

Your parents may need some quiet time to do important paperwork.

Your feelings

If your parents are splitting up, it can be very confusing for you. You might also feel a mix of emotions. Sometimes you may feel sad and lonely. Or confused and worried. You may even feel happier because your parents are not arguing any more. You may worry about the future. You might want to cry more than usual. You may find it harder to concentrate. This is normal.

How do you feel?

 **TIP**

You may be worried about your parents and hide your emotions. But try to be open with them about your feelings. They can try to help you.

It can be hard to concentrate when you are worried or unhappy.

Coping with your feelings

Separation or divorce is a stressful time. It's OK for you to feel sad or hurt. It can be frustrating when your family situation is changing. You may feel that the situation is out of your control. This may make you feel angry.

Many children feel angry when their parents split up.

Taking deep breaths can help you to calm down.

Sometimes it can be hard to cope with your emotions. But it is important that you find a way. If you feel angry, you might want to hit out. But it's not OK to hurt someone else.

Talk about it

Talking about your problems and feelings can help. You will probably have lots of questions about what is happening. Try to talk to your parents or another family member. Or you might want to talk to a trusted adult. Perhaps a teacher or a friend's parent can help.

Sharing a problem can make us feel better about it.

It can help to find out about other people's experiences.

TIP

If your teacher doesn't already know that your family situation is changing, you could ask your parent to tell them. Then they can look out for you and you can talk to them if you're upset.

You might want to talk to your friends about how you feel. You could try talking to a friend whose parents have split up. Perhaps you could go to their house for tea to see what it's like.

Draw it

You might not always feel like talking. It can sometimes be hard to find the right words. If this is how you feel, you could draw or paint a picture instead. Being creative can help you to feel calmer. It can also help you to make sense of your feelings.

Remember, it's OK to feel sad when your family is changing.

TIP

Sometimes it's good to forget about your worries. Do something that makes you feel happy. You could read your favourite book or play with your toys.

You might want to show your picture to your parents. This could help them understand your feelings. Art is a great way to express yourself. It doesn't matter if you're not good at drawing.

▲ Talking about your artwork is a good way to share your feelings with your parents.

19

Write about it

It is good to talk about our feelings. But sometimes we might not want to share them all. Keeping a diary or journal about your feelings may help you. You don't have to write in it every day. Just write in it when you want to.

Writing a journal can help you work out your feelings.

▲ Some people find it helpful to write down their worries. They then rip up the piece of paper and throw away their worries.

You might want to write about how things are going to be in the future too. Perhaps you will be getting a second bedroom. Are there practical plans you can help with?

Can I change it?

You might think that by changing your behaviour, you can bring your parents back together. And as much as you may want to change things, you can't. Parents split up because of problems they have with each other.

Some parents just make each other sad.

You have a right to love both your parents.

It is up to your parents to work out their own issues.
They may still decide living apart is best for everyone.
Remember, your parents still love you. It's not your
fault that they are splitting up.

The future

What will happen to me? It's natural to feel worried about what will happen to you. You may be worried about who you will live with. Or if you will have to move house or go to a different school.

Some children may need to move to a new school when their parents divorce.

▲ Your family will still want to see you.

You may worry about not seeing one of your parents or your grandparents. It can take time to organize things when parents split up. Your parents might not be able to answer all your questions straight away.

Will things change?

Your home life will probably change. You might live most of the time with one parent. You may live with the other parent at the weekend. You may have a new **stepfamily** to get used to.

If your parents live far apart, you may see one of your parents during the school holidays. Or you may divide the holidays between both parents.

▶ You may have new stepbrothers or sisters to play with.

Every family is different but you will get used to the changes. You might even prefer your new home life.

▲ You may find your home life with each parent is quite different.

A new start

If your parents are splitting up, you might feel like life will never be the same again. But you will get used to these changes over time. Talk to your parents about what the future may be like.

Ali and Annie's advice

⭐ Remember, your parents splitting up is not your fault.

⭐ Don't cover up your feelings. It doesn't make them go away.

⭐ Try to share your feelings with someone you trust.

⭐ Everyone feels different. You might have different emotions to your brother or sister.

⭐ Don't take your anger or hurt out on other people.

⭐ Your parents aren't splitting up to hurt you.

⭐ You can keep in touch with each parent by phone or video calls, text messages or emails.

⭐ Ask questions.

⭐ Write a list of ideas for fun things to do with each parent when you are together. Think of things that are indoors and outdoors.

⭐ It will take time to get used to your new home life.

Glossary

court place where legal matters are decided. A family court decides where children are going to live if their parents split up.

emotions feelings

judge person who decides on legal matters, like where a child should live if the parents cannot decide after they have separated

lawyer person who helps people with legal matters, like doing the paperwork for a divorce

legal connected to the law

relationship counsellor person who helps couples to work out their problems

responsibility having the job of taking care of someone or something

stepfamily new family made when a parent marries a new partner

Find out more

Books

The Great Big Book of Families, Mary Hoffman (Lincoln Children's Books, 2015)

The Great Big Book of Feelings, Mary Hoffman (Lincoln Children's Books, 2016)

When Parents Separate (Questions and Feelings about...), Dawn Hewitt (Franklin Watts, 2017)

Websites

www.cafcass.gov.uk/young-people/my-parents-are-separating/

Read stories from children that have already been through divorce and separation.

www.childline.org.uk/info-advice/home-families/family-relationships/divorce-separation/

Learn more ways to cope with divorce and separation at this website.

Index